Table of Contents

YOUR MONEY, YOUR SLAVE
BOOK 1: POWER TO EARN.

Remember the Lord your God! He is the one who gives you the strength to be prosperous in order to establish the covenant he made with your ancestors - and that is how things stand right now.
- Deuteronomy 8:18

Background

In our contemporary societies, people are prone to disagree on almost everything. It seems almost impossible to make a statement or express an opinion without eliciting controversy. A supporter of globalization who actively promotes trade as a means of improving lives and eliminating poverty will find himself pitted against those on the opposite end of the spectrum who provide strong evidence of the adverse effects of globalization in many communities, citing instances of terrorism, job insecurity, currency fluctuation and price instability. If you are a believer in science or an environmental activist who opines that global warming is destroying Mother Earth, you will find, almost everywhere you turn, other groups of people who consider climate change to be an international hoax or insist that it is part of "the natural planetary cycles." They may even question your logic, citing evidence of the extreme cold temperatures that people in cold regions like Toronto often witness during the peak of the Winter season. If you believe that healthcare is a natural human right, and that the provision of universal healthcare by the government is crucial to the ability of the most marginalized segments of any population to live lives of dignity, you will find that there are millions of opposing views to, often vehemently, counter your position. They may tell you that your health is your responsibility and also argue that universal healthcare would lead to increased taxes, reduce funding for other crucial programs, such as defense or education, hinder innovation in the medical field and reduce the flexibility of patients.

The statement "Money is important" is however, indisputable. While it is true that money doesn't buy happiness, no one can deny the fact that money is needed for basic survival. It is a universally accepted fact that money is an awesome tool for society to achieve many of its most important objectives. Money can be a vehicle for attaining independence, satisfying your sense of discovery, and achieving personal fulfillment. With money, we can buy food, pay rent, have fun with friends and family, learn new things, visit new places, make new friends, contribute to an important cause that is larger than us, and make the good things in our lives even better. Financial security is so important that parents spend billions of dollars yearly to equip their children with post-secondary degrees, which are expected to give them the opportunity to pursue higher paying careers, redesign their futures and attain a decent standard of living. Money is so vital, that billions of people all over the world wake up every day, to prepare for work, traverse often great distances to get to work, expend themselves mentally and physically to stay productive even when they are not mentally inspired, and navigate various challenges along the way, all so that, at the end of the month, they can earn some money to support their existence and lifestyle.

Before we begin, I need you to entirely disabuse yourself of the notion that money is 'the' goal. If you believe that money will solve all of your problems and define it as your saving grace, you are already facing a losing battle. Money is a tool, which can be utilized to fulfill your wants and needs. When you see money as your servant and learn to deploy it humanely, it will serve you, benefit your society, and create a win-win environment that everyone will be proud to be a part of.

Our contemporary societies are characterized by a striking predisposition to value material possessions even higher than human life. Advances in technology and civilization are seemingly attended by a corresponding prevalence of acquisitiveness and avarice, to the point where it seems that greed has completely taken the society over. Everywhere you turn, the prevailing narrative is that of "winner-takes-all" and "dog-eats-dog". The rich keep getting richer, the middle class are a few paychecks from sliding below the poverty line, and the poor have little to no hope of ever getting ahead in life. It is a society where elected politicians choose to serve the entrenched self-interest of their donors and the special interest groups that financed their elections, rather than to advance the cause of the electorate. These days, an average CEO makes 300 times the salary of the average employee in his organization. Factors like globalization, disruptive technologies, and the decline of organized labor are forcing the income inequality gap into a seemingly unbridgeable chasm. Politicians have proven ineffective at reining in the menace of the ever-widening income gap that has pervaded our culture, and which has gradually become the norm around us. The society is now starkly divided between the very rich and the extremely poor, with the shrinking middle-class right in the center.

The last decade has witnessed increasing numbers of people dropping out of the mainstream drive for economic success. Many people believe the system is rigged against them and have increasingly resorted to hating (despising) the wealthy as a means of dealing with their lack of opportunities. This is further exacerbated by the prevalent trend in dynasticism where the leaders of industry and politics groom their often mediocre children to continue their political and economic domination while talented children from less affluent families rarely make significant inroads. Furthermore, the politicians actively participate in the dangerous trend by instituting government policies that continue to broaden the gap and by encouraging politically charged rhetoric which exploits the apparent lack of opportunities to further divide the society.

You relinquish your power when you lose control of your emotions. Giving way to corrosive emotional patterns like anger, hatred, or envy, will not move you one step closer to resolving the prevalent issue, which is lack of money. Knowledge, education, and courage will. The knowledge of how money works, the education to know the difference between assets and liabilities, and the courage to make a practical plan to guide you through the process of earning, saving, investing, and thriving with your money is what you need to build the life you desire.

This book will share practical life lessons to guide you as you become more intentional with your money and help you lay the groundwork for financial success and sound money management skills. You will also learn to identify the money mistakes that you must avoid in order to achieve financial freedom.

I have divided the Money Quadrant Series into four volumes, which will equip you with vital knowledge and skills in **"Earning"**, **"Saving"**, **"Investing"** and **"Thriving"**. The first book in the series titled "The Power to Earn", will teach you how to make money, equip you with the skills you need to achieve financial mastery and help you identify and deploy your passions to achieve your financial goals and fulfill your dreams for a better life. You will learn the true value of money and confront the tricky question of 'just how much money is enough?' This book will make you the master of your money and help you take back your power. When you recognize that money is your slave, you will put it back in its rightful place as a tool that must be consciously applied to fulfill your needs. Get ready for a mind-shift!

Who This Book Is For

Most of us have had to struggle with money at some point in our lives. If you   grew up watching your parents fight over money-related issues, have ever been worried about money or are struggling with your financial situation, this book is for you. If you have spent your life watching people around you constantly grappling with money issues and you want your financial reality to be different from the norm, this book will teach you to master your money and grow your income exponentially.

Do you struggle with debt? Despite of a decent income, do you have a hard time paying your monthly expenses? Do you find it hard to stretch your income to last through the entire month? If you answer 'yes' to any of these questions, this book is the instruction manual you need to figure out and solve your money issues. Regardless of your level of financial expertise, lack of training in money management or how much money you have in your bank account, this book will give you a better grasp of your finances, take you on the next steps towards financial freedom and will become your trusted Money Guide for **growing your income, saving smart, reducing debt, budgeting the smart way, investing your money**, and living the life you've always desired.

CHAPTER 1

1.0   Understanding the Act of Earning.

Recently, I attended a seminar where the subject of how to make money was discussed. One of the seminar participants rose up and emphatically opined that *"everyone must become a business-owner"*. In her words, *"if you don't own your own business, you are a slave to your employer"*. While I disagree with the finer points of this statement, I am inclined to agree with the sentiment in a more holistic sense. In a world that is ever-changing, where job security is as fleeting as a bubble, can anyone really ensure that they will always have a job that provides a guaranteed income stream from month to month for the entire duration of their career? The crucial question then remains: is there anything that you, as an individual, can do to ensure that you continuously earn money and keep your income streams flowing?

The truth is, owning your business does not guarantee income for life. Having a thriving business can provide a clear and steady path towards financial freedom, but we must also recognize that many start-ups struggle financially and there are many struggling business owners. A large number of startups that start off as being profitable are unable to sustain the business for the long haul, while many new businesses never quite get off the ground. According to the Small Business Association (SBA) estimates, over 627,000 new businesses open in the United States each year, while about 595,000 businesses will close within the same time frame. Also, data from the US Bureau of Labor Statistics reveal that about 20% of businesses fail in their first year, about 50% of small businesses fail in their fifth year, and only around 30% of businesses will survive their 10th year in business. The available statistics reveal a rather grim prospect for small businesses and show that while there are risks involved with earning money as an employee, a business owner will potentially face a number of income uncertainties as well.

Financial responsibility is widely recognized as one of the hallmarks of adulthood. To be considered responsible, an adult is expected to find and sustain a means of earning an income. The good news is that various tools and avenues are now widely available to use your skills, knowledge, talent, education, assets, or money to earn a sustainable income. For example, a doctor uses his professional experience to nurture his patients to health and earns an income in the process. The local farmer, who supplies groceries to the flea market, tills the ground and exerts his physical strength and abilities to make a living. The college professor gets paid by using her mental abilities to educate her students, write treatises and delivers lectures in the classroom. Dancers, actors, singers, and comedians use their creative abilities to entertain the audience and earn a living from it. The passionate lawyer in the courtroom uses his training and experience by advocating for his clients to earn an income. The small business-owner who fixes broken computers also gets paid for offering services to his clients.

The contemporary business landscape and the corresponding technological innovations provide increased opportunities to make a sustainable income. Interestingly, the innovative guy who creates an app that allows these traditional service providers interface more easily with their clients, the YouTuber who creates content that helps these professionals refine their skills and the influencer who uses his platform to stimulate social commentary and highlight the trends and innovations in these fields are also able to create viable income streams.

1.1   Know your Income Quadrant

INCOME QUADRANT	
EMPLOYEE	INVESTOR
SELF-EMPLOYED	BUSINESS OWNER

Table 1: Income Quadrant

The moment you begin to make money, your income will fall into one of the four categories in the Income Quadrant table shown above. No matter who you are or what you do, you can achieve your goal of financial freedom from any of the quadrants as long as you understand how money works. Naturally, the focus is on people with legitimate sources of income, and our strategies will not apply to those who make their money through illegal means, Ponzi schemes, pyramid schemes, or other get-rich-quick schemes. If what you do is legitimate, you can raise your head up high and be comfortable to earn within your chosen quadrant(s).

The pervasive myth surrounding the status of an employee in our culture has conditioned most people to believe that no one can become truly wealthy as an employee. I differ with this opinion, and consider it to be a myopic point of view. Can you imagine a world where everyone decides to become an entrepreneur in their own right? In this utopian world, each doctor will have his own practice, the laundromat down the street will probably have to close down because there are no longer any customers. A trip to the licensing office to renew your driver's license will not be necessary because there will be no one there to help you out. Our metro and public transportation systems will be shut down for lack of drivers. Most factories would be closed down due to the absence of factory workers. There will also be no one available to build cars, buses, and trucks! It is quite apparent that this cannot be anyone's desired world. There is an age-old dignity in working which gives the worker satisfaction at being a part of the process of up-building and advancement of that which already exists. There is a certain strength in numbers and you do not become less of a man or woman if you earn your living as an employee. The important factor here is to ensure that what you do brings you personal fulfillment and satisfaction, and can meet your needs.

1.2   Active and Passive Income

It is clear that you can earn your income legally from a variety of professions. Having said that, one important factor which distinguishes the super wealthy from your average *Joe Six-Pack* neighbor is that the rich have mastered the art of income streaming and are proficient at finding creative ways to earn their income from multiple sources. Just as there are many different positions out there for you to tap into, there are also multiple sources available for you to earn your income. In my own case, I went to college to learn Engineering and a large chunk of my income is earned in my capacity as an engineer. This is known as active income. Active income is income received for performing a service. This includes salaries, wages, tips and commissions, and involves dedicating time to an endeavor on a continuous basis in order to earn an income from it. In order to diversify my earning portfolio, I generate additional income from multiple sources, which include my books, my mentorship and coaching business, ownership of stocks, and rental income from my investment properties.

The income that I receive for my work as an engineer is an Active Income. If I do not work, I do not get paid. On the other hand, the money that I make from my investment in shares and real estate is passive income. Passive Income is the money that I make for doing (almost) nothing. I get this money every month, or quarterly, as long as I have tenants, or the businesses that I invest in are doing well. Passive income is the type of income that you earn when you make your money work for you. This often involves a one-time investment, such as the initial amount that I invested to acquire a real estate property or to buy shares in a company. Other forms of passive income may require extensive effort to begin with, such as the income that I earn as an author. It may take hundreds of hours to write my first book, but once the book is completed, I do not have to put any more time into this endeavor to continue earning an income from my book.

Passive income is the gift that keeps on giving. The best path to building a wealthy life is to ensure that you continue to create avenues and opportunities to keep your passive income on an upward growth trajectory. The point where your passive income exceeds your active income is a point where you can attain financial freedom, assuming your active income is sufficient to sustain and support your desired standard of living. When you begin to take conscious and deliberate steps to build a passive income portfolio, the process may be initially slow, except in cases where you receive a windfall or start off with a large sum of money which gives you a head start in your journey to financial wellbeing. As a newbie investor, my first investment was in stocks. I invested about $500 to buy 10 units of Bank of America shares, and in return I received $6.40 quarterly dividends. This was my first lesson in the potentiality of passive income. While $6.40 quarterly dividends may seem like an insignificant figure, it was an important turning point in that I learned that I could boost my earnings within a few years if

I increased my investment in the company's shares. I knew that I was looking at a potentially powerful wealth generation source!

Just as with any project that you start from scratch, your ability to stay in touch with your original motive and keep your goals in perspective will help you appreciate the little successes and keep you focused on the bigger picture as you continue to increase your passive income. When I started my career, I knew I had to build my passive income, but I also had to overcome many distractions, chief of which was my desire to do too many different things at the same time. As I learnt to successfully navigate this sphere, I met many other investors who had made similar mistakes and gotten side-tracked when they began their journey to building a successful passive income portfolio. The inspiration behind this book came from my desire to use my experiences as a leverage to help others avoid the same mistakes I made by teaching them how to identify the most profitable passive income streams to focus on, develop the discipline to pile on years of consistent investment and exercise the patience to nurture their investments till they begin to achieve significant progress.

The Power to Earn is founded on your ability to not only work for money, but to make money work even harder for you. When it comes to earning money, most people fall within three categories. There are the 'under-earners' whose income is not commensurate to the skills and abilities they deploy. There are the 'over-earners', who get paid more than they deserve, which typically leads to poor handling and mismanagement of money. And then, right in the middle is the category that most of us are used to being in, the earning space where you earn what you deserve based on the perceived value of the services you render.

If you are not earning as much as you deserve, then you should strongly consider changing your trajectory. As an employee, this could involve looking for another job that pays higher. Similarly, business owners can change their growth trajectory by working hard to attract more customers, which could be achieved by diversifying their business, specializing in niche areas or improving the quality of their services. Of course, changing jobs or switching careers is usually a demanding and tricky process, but I will strongly encourage you to develop the mindset to never settle for less than you are worth in life. That is the attitude of winners! Yes, you could hold on to that job, but make sure that it is only for a temporary period, and in the meantime, do whatever you can to look for a better opportunity and position yourself to attract it. You can do this by learning new skills, investing in specialized courses, getting further education by enrolling in part-time, online degree programs, or as a matter of fact, starting a side business where you can earn some money to supplement your income. The modern innovations in technology have made it easy to start up a business, and anyone can leverage on one original and creative idea to build a successful business. Your dreams are valid and you surely have what it takes to make them a reality, so don't ever tell yourself anything less. It may take some time, effort and intentionality, but you can come up with an idea that will be the key to enhancing your income and living the good life you've always dreamed of.

CHAPTER 2

2.0   Life Energy Concept

I have two great friends, Kevin and Kelvin. We often get together to discuss the important issues of life. We talk openly about our careers, marriages, families, raising children, businesses, vacations, and of course, money issues. Over the years, we have become advisers to each other and often consult one another whenever one of us is faced with serious and consequential life decisions. The three of us are hardworking, dedicated and devoted fathers with strong family values. Kevin is a successful Vice President in one of the top banks in the country while Kelvin works as a Data Analyst with a local IT company. They both enjoy their respective careers and are top performers in their respective organizations. Kevin's annual earnings are around $250,000 per annum, including bonuses, while Kelvin's total package is around $147,000.

These two men work hard to take care of their families, but from my conversations with them, I noticed that even though Kevin's income places him among the top 5% earners in America, he is still not fulfilled. He often feels sad because he is unable to make sufficient time to be available for his family. His position in his organization puts a lot of stress on him and places a high demand on his time. He usually works fifteen to seventeen hours daily. He is usually unable to make it to his children's school events and sports activities, and almost always, by the time he gets home in the evening, the kids are already in bed. His commitment at the office has put a lot of strain on his personal relationships.

Whenever I have discussions with him when he shares the pressures and challenges that he grapples with in order to balance his professional and personal commitments, it draws my mind to the concept of Life Energy. Life Energy is measured based on the number of hours that you expend to earn your income. It is true that Kevin earns a lot more than Kelvin when you only factor in the take home pay. However, the moment you begin to consider the hours it takes or the life energy expended on earning their respective incomes, the story becomes conspicuously different.

2.1   Life Energy Calculation

Kevin
Kevin earns $250,000 per annum
Kevin expends an average of 80 hours every week at work.
Kevin expends an average of 4,160 hours annually at work.

$$\textbf{Life Energy} = \frac{Total\ Income}{Total\ Hours\ Expended}$$

Kevin's Life Energy $= \frac{250,000}{4,160} = \$60/\text{hour}$

This means, when the time spent working is taken into consideration, Kevin earns $60/hour.

Kelvin
Kelvin earns $147,000 per annum
Kelvin expends an average of 40 hours every week at work.
Kelvin expends an average of 2,080 hours annually at work.

Kelvin's Life Energy $= \frac{147,000}{2,080} = \$70.67/\text{hour}$

This means, when the time spent working is taken into consideration, Kelvin earns about $70/hour.

Many people don't necessarily consider the hours they will expend at work when they accept offers from a potential employer, but this is an important consideration that can change the way you earn your money and transmute your resources. From the analysis above, even though Kevin earns a higher salary than Kelvin, from the Life Energy standpoint, Kelvin is the higher earner.

If you do not fully understand the concept of Life Energy, it helps to think about it this way. You would like to buy a fuel-efficient vehicle, and you have told the car dealer what you are looking for. You have taken your time to describe the particular features you want – leather seats, a back-up camera, a self-parking device, a tire pressure alert system, and an efficient navigation system. The dealer gives you two options that meet your needs but with different levels of fuel consumption. Car A will use up 30 gallons for every 100 miles driven, while Car B will only consume 10 gallons for the same distance. Which of the two cars will you consider more efficient? I bet you will choose Car B! You chose based on fuel efficiency, which was your primary objective. You must learn to apply the same concept to your career when evaluating your earning potential, provided that all other factors remain the same.

You should ensure that you are earning efficiently by adequately balancing your personal and professional commitments. Kevin's high salary comes at a high cost to his personal life. He does not get to spend sufficient time with his family, he is usually unable to attend his children's games, he travels frequently, and most of the time, he is seriously stressed out. In order to meet his targets, he often brings work home and on those rare weekends when he is not away from home, he spends most of his time on the phone discussing business strategies or helping to make important business decisions. Kevin is making daily sacrifices that cannot be quantified easily in terms of monetary values.

Kevin's story is similar to the story of many business owners that I've met in my career. The bigger the businesses grow and the more successful they become, the more time they have to commit to growing their business, often at the expense of other important things in their lives, including their health, families, and personal time. This is not a healthy way to earn money. Making money should not be at all costs, and should not come by sacrificing the essential things in your life. The Power to Earn is about knowing the right income base to sustain your personal and family needs, knowing the type of jobs to go after, and mastering how to balance your personal and professional responsibilities.

ACTIVITY

TASK: Determine your life energy

STEPS:
1. What is the total income you receive from your employer?

2. How many hours do you spend on average every month to earn your salary?
3. Establish your life energy by dividing your total income by the total hours spent to earn it.

   Question to ponder: Are you happy with your income based on the time you spend to earn it? Do you deserve more or less?

CHAPTER 3

3.0   The Five Commandments of Earning Money

I have had the opportunity to interact with people from diverse backgrounds. I've listened to Julia, a hard-working single mother who earns minimum wage and struggles to make ends meet, pay rent and bills, and put food on the table for her family. Julia was stuck in her job, needing to work extra hours in order to bring more money home, but this always came at a huge cost to her two small children.

I also know Jason, a young business executive at a startup in San Francisco, California. Jason's total package is a little above $1M every year. He is married and has one son. Jason is a prolific earner, but he is not very good when it comes to managing his money. He is quite extravagant, lives in an upper-class neighborhood, drives exotic cars, sends his children to expensive private schools, and racks up a high credit card balance every month. Jason spends as he earns and is nonchalant about saving for retirement. According to him, "*I am a high-income earner, it is easy enough for me to plan and save for retirement within five years of my retirement day.*"

Then there's Tanya. Tanya and her husband are both middle-income earners in America. Tanya works as a Sales Manager in the food and beverage industry, while her husband, Mike, is a Science teacher in a public high school. This family is very disciplined with their money. They have a monthly budget to help plan their income, they are both saving towards retirement, and they plan to pay for their children's college tuition by contributing to the 529 College Education Plan. Tanya and Mike live in a decent neighborhood, and they take family vacations, once in every two years. They have learned how to master their money game by carefully allocating their income to those things that are important to them. Tanya and Mike are quite frugal with their money, and they avoid debt as much as possible. They are already on track to paying their mortgage off early, and they are not even in their 40's yet. They have confidence that the money they are saving in their 401k Plan will be more than sufficient for them when they are ready for retirement. Tanya and Mike are the perfect example of those millionaires next door that you are quick to overlook because their lifestyle does not necessarily match their net worth.

What is the difference between Julia, Jason, & Tanya? Julia is an under-earner who struggles to take care of her two daughters with the meager income she earns. Jason is a high-income earner who lacks financial goals, is reckless and prone to mismanaging money. Tanya is a middle-income earner, who is disciplined with her income, and as such, is on track to achieving financial freedom. She is competent with money management, and she has peace with her finances. Tanya understands the basic rules of earning money, managing money and maximizing money.

At some point in our working lives, most of us have asked ourselves these questions:

'Can anyone achieve financial peace?'

'Can we all learn the rules of earning money?'

'Why do some people earn so much, and yet, they constantly struggle with managing their money?'

'How come some people remain under-earners, living on minimum wage all through their careers?'

'Is there anything that can be done to ensure that more people earn what they deserve?'

The answer to all these questions lies in the understanding and conscientious practice of some immutable principles or commandments.

THE FIRST COMMANDMENT: KNOWLEDGE IS MONEY:

Our Heavenly Father loves us so much that He has deposited unique talents in each one of us. He also empowers us to use these talents for the benefit of humankind, and to our individual advantage. One of the most common ways to transmute talent or knowledge is to use it to make money. Doctors go to college to acquire knowledge in

17

Medicine. Engineers acquire knowledge by learning about engineering designs and practices. After graduating from college, the next logical step for most people is to apply for a job where they can get the chance to apply the knowledge they have acquired. Even if you would like to pursue other paths rather than jumping right into a nine-to-five, full-time career as an employee, you will still need to gain relevant work experience in your field in order to apply your knowledge and create a means of earning an income with it. This will be a great jumping off point to help you decide how to use the hard skills you have to create a new career path by inventing a novel, groundbreaking product or deciding to provide some services that will benefit others.

It is noteworthy that, while it can open a lot of doors, having a college degree is not the only way to earn money. Some of the most successful people in business and the Arts are college dropouts, while many more did not attend college at all. If you do not have a college degree, it is important to know that you also possess the knowledge and power you need to earn money and create wealth. The crucial factor is to know who you are, what you enjoy and what you are great at doing.

For each person, the most important task is to discover a way to use their skills, talents, and knowledge to create something that will benefit others, and in return, make money. The more useful their products or services are to others, the more money they can make from these ventures. Elon Musk is a typical example of a visionary man whose knowledge and affinity for technology was used to start companies like Tesla and SpaceX, which create products that many people find beneficial, and are willing to pay a lot of money to use. Robert Kiyosaki's best-selling book, 'Rich Dad, Poor Dad', is a direct product of the application of Robert's knowledge and life experiences gained while navigating personal finance and business. He wrote the book, which became one of the best-selling personal finance books in the world, and as a result, millions of readers around the world attained financial literacy and learned to manage their money.

When it comes to earning money, you need to be intentional. You can apply the knowledge you learned in college to earn income as an employee. You can deploy your creative or physical skills to make money, as many professional athletes, musicians, dancers and comedians do. You can execute an idea by starting a business to fill a particular need in the market. You can become an investor by putting your money into a project or business, and in return, you make money if the project is successful. If you are not deliberate about your process and choose to do nothing about your situation, nothing will change.

The first commandment of the Power to Earn states that:

"you must apply your skills, talents, and knowledge to create a product or service that will be of benefit to others".

Most people are falling behind in the game of money simply because of their inability to transmute their knowledge into earnings.

THE SECOND COMMANDMENT: DON'T BE A SLAVE TO MONEY:

Many people work very hard for money. They believe that the harder and longer they work, the more money they can potentially earn. Many of these people have multiple jobs and work around the clock trying to make ends meet; yet, they often find themselves living paycheck to paycheck. People who understand the concept of Power to Earn do the opposite. They work smart, not hard, by letting money work for them. Money is a tool, your slave, and if deployed properly with care and caution, it can bring even more money to you. Countries all over the world recognize the negative effect of the widening income gap, which is exacerbating the disparity between the haves and the have-nots, but often, they are powerless in reversing this trend. If they were to increase the minimum wage, the cost of items, and subsequently, the inflation rates, will rise drastically, which will mean a return to the status quo. In such a scenario, a person who previously earned wages of $8 per hour will still have the same buying power when the minimum wage is increased to $15 per hour. The rationale behind this is that an increase in the minimum wage will be passed on to consumers through price increases. This will also hurt businesses and lead to job losses and unemployment for the working poor, thereby slowing spending and economic growth. Consequently, the Government is always wary of increasing minimum wage because of the overall effect it can have on the nation's economy.

In terms of earning money, the government has an important role to play in that they need to build a thriving economy where there is upward mobility in income for the citizens. The truth is that most administrations have been ineffective at attaining this feat, and the current economy is one that enshrines the survival of the fittest. What this means is that some people may have to leave their home town or country to look for opportunities in a different location in order to earn an income that is sufficient to sustain the lifestyle they desire. Some people will have to invest in post-graduate degrees or acquire specialized certifications in order to get a higher paying job. Some other people will choose to stick with their minimum wage jobs and augment their income by combining it with (two or more) other jobs. Others will simply depend on the government to take care of their needs. Working two or more jobs is not the solution you need to attain your full earning potential as it will keep you overstretched, overstressed and take away the quality time you could have for other important things in life. It is a way of working hard, not smart for your money, and invariably, it is a surefire way to become a slave to your money.

Money is important, but your time is precious too. Do not slave away at jobs that will barely help you attain your desired standard of living. It is okay to compromise when you are just starting out and need to work for less than you know you deserve in order to gain the experience you need, but do not stay too long at a low paying job. Doing that will position you to become a lifetime under-achiever and under-earner. You need to ask yourself: *'what, specifically, do I need to do to get to the next level?'* Look for a mentor or role model that has transcended the odds you now face and is willing to guide you to that next level, and consciously apply the life and career lessons they transmit to you.

The Second Commandment of Power To Earn states that:

"you must explore ways to earn the income you deserve".

It is counterproductive to continue to waste away and slave away at a low paying job. Although money is important, your time is also precious. You must avoid spending all your time looking for money at the expense of the other important things in your life including your family, friends, fun, relaxation and self-care/vacation time for yourself.

THE THIRD COMMANDMENT: IMPROVE YOUR EARNING POWER BY ADDING VALUE

This rule helps you become a more valuable person. The more value you can add, whether as a business owner or as an employee, the higher the income you can potentially command. This is the reason why companies pay an engineer with 20 years of experience much more than they pay a wet-behind-the-ears Engineer that is fresh out of college. Some people often find it absurd that the super-rich make as much money as they do. For example, it was estimated that Jeff Bezos, the richest man on earth, earns close to $2,500 every single second based on his net worth. What many people don't realize is that Jeff Bezos was able to build an e-commerce juggernaut with his company, Amazon, which constantly adds value to people's lives by giving them an awesome shopping experience and consistently providing services which make life easier for its customers. With millions of visitors every month, Amazon has become a household name for a diverse range of products that customers can easily buy from the comfort of their homes at a very competitive price, and have delivered at their doorstep within one or two days. Using this business model, Amazon was able to disrupt the traditional brick and mortar stores, which required people to visit their stores in order to make purchases.

In an ideal society, your income level is tied to the value you bring to the table. As an individual, you can add value to your employer by helping them reduce costs, eliminate waste, or develop processes that will boost productivity. You can also increase your value and increase your earning power by obtaining industry certifications, advanced degrees, or getting specialized trainings that will help you improve your skills. To advance in your career, you must continuously and creatively find ways to improve your earning power.

To recap, the third commandment of earning money states that

"you must seek to improve your earning power by increasing the value of service that you give to your employer or customers".

THE FOURTH COMMANDMENT: BE A WEALTH MAGNET

Your Financial Magnetism Quotient (FMQ) is measured based on your ability to attract money. Your ability to become a wealth magnet begins with your attitude and mindset about money. The common factor with most people who do not earn as much as they work for or deserve is they have held negative beliefs about money for far too long. They believe that money is synonymous with evil, that they can never have enough, that they will always be broke, that they will always be on minimum wage or hold similarly limiting beliefs about money. For some people, being rich and being pious are mutually exclusive events. These negative beliefs and 'lack' mentality have placed an imaginary bar on their aspirations, setting a natural limit to how far they can grow and consequently how much they can earn.

Power to Earn requires you to break negative belief patterns and embrace the 'Abundance' mindset. A mindset that is devoid of limitations, which recognizes your ability to earn what you deserve, is the right attitude to attract and retain more of your income. To become a wealth magnet, you must have the right attitude about money. You must recognize the fact that you can always improve your earning capability by meeting certain conditions, and stand in the conviction that your wealth must be used as a tool for service, that is, a part of your earnings must be given out to bless others and lift them up.

By becoming more generous, you position yourself to attract more opportunities that will empower you to attract more wealth. It may seem difficult to tell a person that lives paycheck to paycheck to become more generous, but the truth is, by looking at your situation, you will find out that your condition is better off than that of at least a billion other people around the world. I know that because you have access to this book. There are some places in the world where people still struggle to get clean water or electricity to power their homes, and where many people survive on less than a dollar a day. In the end, it is about developing a character trait that positions you to attract abundance.

On your path to sustainable wealth, it is important to find a way to give back to those who lack certain benefits that you enjoy or to support charities whose causes are close to your heart. If you are not at the financial level that you'd like to inhabit yet, ensure that you do not hate on those who are financially better off than you are. Don't detest them, don't call them names, and don't be over-critical of their successes. Rather, you should find a way to learn what they've done right, find out how they have accumulated their wealth and use their example as a catalyst to discover the strategies you need to apply to improve your own earning capacity. You must also take care to avoid dangerous money repellants, such as addictions, divorce and wasteful spending, which are capable of harming you financially or even leading to financial ruin.

The fourth commandment of earning money states that:

'you must attract money to yourself'.

You obey this commandment when you are deliberate about fostering favorable money beliefs and maintaining a positive attitude towards those who have more than you do as well as those who have less than you do. To be a wealth magnet, you must be strategic with your earning, avoid being an under-earner for too long, avoid money repellents and ensure that you are always in a good position to earn at the desired level.

THE FIFTH COMMANDMENT: ESTABLISH YOUR ENOUGH

Is it possible to get to a point when you will no longer need to work actively, but will still earn a steady income? Does this idea seem far-fetched to you? Do you think it is crazy when someone tells you that, at a certain point in their life, they will not need to work actively anymore, but money will keep rolling into their account from month to month? If this scenario sounds unbelievable to you in any way, then I need to introduce a colleague of mine to you.

Chris R. graduated from high school in 1980 and earned his GED whilst working at a local plastics manufacturing company. He later joined the Army reserves and during that period, continued to learn and improve his skills as a manufacturing technician. Chris was about 56 years old when I met him. I found him to be a methodical and dedicated person, and it was obvious that he thoroughly enjoyed his work. Due to some re-organization efforts in his company, Chris' boss was transferred to a different unit in the organization. The new boss had a managerial style which made him difficult to work with. He was extremely controlling, prone to micromanaging his team, and rarely gave anyone room to make decisions without double checking with him.

Many of Chris' colleagues constantly complained about this manager, although they were resigned to fate and usually agreed that nothing could be done to rectify the situation. Chris, however, was not bothered by the temperament of his new manager. I was curious to know why he was so relaxed and calm when the people around him were anxious and panicky. During one of our conversations, I asked why he was unfazed with his new boss. He told me, 'because *I have a date*'. '*What date*?' I asked, as my curiosity grew even more intense. '*My "have to, want to" date*', he retorted.

According to him, when he started working, he knew that active working must have an end date, and he planned to empower himself to dictate the day that he will make the decision to stop working. He called the date, his '*have to, want to*' date. According to him, the major question he asks himself is whether he is working because he *has to* or because he *wants to*. He explained that his goal from Day One at the company was to quickly get to his "*want-to date*". By this date, he would have accumulated enough money to support his lifestyle without needing to continue to work for money. Chris did not just pick an arbitrary date or income as his "*enough*"; rather, he arrived at those numbers based on careful planning, deliberate strategy, and persistent focus. These helped him stay on course to achieve his goal of retiring early.

For most people, the *"enough"* is the day that they are no longer able to work due to age restrictions or unforeseen circumstances, but this shouldn't be the case. I believe that everyone must begin to think about their *"enough"* date as soon as they begin their career, and that retirement should actually be based on *the "enough"*, and not on the individual's age. If you attain the *"enough"* at age 50, for example, you can then ask yourself the magic question – *'do I still want to work?'* It is noteworthy that you must take care to ensure that you are not over-projecting the income from your investments. You must also be careful to factor uncertainties into your estimate before deciding to continue to work or to stop working.

Many people are prepared to work until they reach the retirement age, or they die. Some people keep working because they were unable to get to their *"enough"*. Some keep working out of greed, accumulating more and more, even when they are well past their *"enough"* level. There are also others who continue to work simply because they are not sure what is sufficient to take care of their needs. Not working actively is not equivalent to a dearth in your capacity to earn an income once you stay creative and ensure that your money is always working for you. In Chapter Three of this book, I will teach you all you need to know to generate passive income by making your money work hard for you.

The Fifth Commandment of Earning states that,

"as you work to earn money, you must ensure that you establish a target income that is considered 'enough' for you, such that when you reach that target, you can decide whether or not you still want to work actively".

3.1   Mistakes to Avoid when Earning Money

Many people are unable to earn as much as they desire because of the lack of adequate opportunities around them. Many people are hindered by a tight job market, unfriendly business climate, and unfavorable government policies that discourage and stifle innovation and creativity in citizens. If you are in a situation where you don't earn as much as you need to maintain the lifestyle you want, the motivation that I have for you is to never give up and accept this condition. Accepting your current circumstances is tantamount to throwing in the towel and believing that you are powerless to change your circumstances. Take it from me, that is never the case. Unless you choose to admit defeat, you always have everything you need to make a change, control your destiny and build your own business empire. The secret is not to settle for a life that you do not desire. In business, people usually get as much as they are hungry for, so the higher your dreams are, the further up you are able to climb. The best way to jumpstart your goals is to develop a plan, and act on your plans every day until you achieve your goals.

We have spoken about the principles you need to learn and apply to get your financial life in order. While these principles are not rocket science, many people find it difficult to put in the time, energy, and effort they need to achieve their financial objectives. Many high-income earners are similarly unable to position themselves correctly to build lasting wealth. Do you ever wonder why this is so? In order to build lasting wealth, you need to adopt some lifestyle positions, mindsets, and attitudes. However, these people are prone to making multiple money mistakes and fostering ineffective financial habits with their income. In this section, we will reveal the money management mistakes you must avoid in order to build wealth and take control of your future.

1.   **Money-at-all-Costs:**
     Everyone should aim to earn as much as possible to support their needs and maintain a good lifestyle. However, this does not mean, that you should sacrifice other valuable things in your life on the altar of money. When you chase money for money's sake, you tend

to subvert your true values and relegate the very things that bring you lasting fulfillment and make you feel alive – fun, friends, family, and relaxation. 'Money-at-all–Costs' means chasing money at the expense of everything else in your life. It means putting money first. This is why someone will choose a $100 per hour job which may involve exposure to unsafe conditions over another job which offers $60 per hour without the risk factor. What is the most important thing to you? Your money or your life?

Yes, you surely deserve to earn as much as you can, but do not chase money at the expense of your life. When it comes to making a living, your overall priority should be to seek a better work-life balance and flexible working rather than earning heaps of money. I once had a friend who worked on an offshore oil platform. Let's call him Jack[1]. Jack was a hardworking man who made lots of money from his job. He could afford to buy the good things of life for his loved ones. However, he frequently felt unfulfilled. He believed that he had to work hard to take care of his family, but he was unhappy because the work often took him away from his family. He was hardly present in the home, was not there for his wife when she needed him and his children saw him as an absentee father. One day, his first son approached him, and begged him to attend his school debate, which was an event organized as part of the school's "bring your Dad to school" program. Jack turned the boy down with the usual excuse that he had to be at work. On getting to work, he felt bad about his decision and made plans to surprise his son by attending the event.

Unknown to Jack, his son had made alternative arrangements with a neighbor, who agreed to attend the event in Jack's place. On the day of the event, it was a huge embarrassment when Jack showed up for his son, only to find out that someone else has already arrived to represent him. He sat at the back of the auditorium, desolate and ashamed, as he realized that his absenteeism was destroying his relationship with his family. This event affected Jack so much that he decided to make a change. He knew he had to stop living for work, but rather, to begin to work to live. He changed his job two months after the incident, and took a pay cut as a result. He knew he had recognized, before it became too late, that his presence, and the time

---

[1] Not real name

he spent with his loved ones, was something that money couldn't buy.

Are you also chasing money at all costs? You need to make a change, because moments and time with your loved ones cannot be valued in monetary terms, and once lost, they cannot be retrieved.

2. **<u>Thinking that Active Income can last forever:</u>**
Technology is disrupting the world at an alarming rate. We live in an era where job security is fleeting and the good old pension system is gradually becoming obsolete. When you start working, it is important to give it your all and work as if it is the only thing you will ever do, without forgetting that it can end at any time. With that mentality, you will be able to manage your money properly.

When you are conscious of the fact that your active income will not last forever, you are more inclined to do all you can to protect your income. The financial crisis of 2007-08 and the recent Coronavirus pandemic are perfect examples of big shifts in the working world that exemplify the need to understand and accept that job security does not really exist anymore, and that an unexpected event can easily disrupt your source of income either as an employee or a business owner. These milestone events have had a catastrophic effect on working hours and earnings globally as millions of employees have lost their jobs, and many small businesses have had to close down.

When you start working and earning income, it is your duty to build your passive income portfolio, because active income can't and won't last forever, but passive income can give you some guaranteed income for life, with little to no effort required to keep it coming.

3. **<u>Lack of Proper Accountability:</u>**
One of the biggest tasks that you must confront as you earn money is to ensure that you properly plan and manage your money. Lack of accountability in money management is one of the reasons why many people struggle to build wealth. For example, it is expected that an individual who earns $50,000 per year for ten years should be able to save at least $50,000 in those years going by a saving rate

of 10% of his annual income. This seems quite apparent, but the reality is quite different. From my observations, many people work really hard but they have nothing to show for it in the way of savings or investments.

To be accountable for your salary means to judiciously allocate every cent of it towards your financial priorities. At the very top of your priority list must be saving a part of your income, before you allocate money for your expenses. Your accumulated savings will eventually form the foundation on which your wealth will be built.

Later on in this book series, you will learn more about saving and investing. The new generation, particularly the millennials, have led the charge in aggressive saving by allocating a higher percentage of their income towards saving and investing, and cutting down on their living expenses. The younger millennials got the benefit of learning from older millennials who bore the brunt of the financial crisis. They arrived early at the awareness of the risks of a bad economy, which made them more cautious and practical in dealing with money, and encouraged them to save for emergencies, contribute to a retirement accounts and band together in groups like the Frugality Movement, FIRE (Financial Independence, Retire Early), to achieve their goals of financial freedom.

4. **Staying at a Dead-End Job:**
   Your job dictates the Active Income you earn. It is important to ensure that you have available opportunities for career advancement wherever you work. Each year, an average American can get between 2% to 5% pay raise from his/her employer. On the other hand, employees who change roles or move to a different company can have an average of 10% to 15% increase in their salary. If you stay too long in a position where career growth opportunities and advancement are limited, you are hurting your chances of climbing higher up the corporate ladder and earning a higher income.

If you work in a company that does not present a clear path for career growth, you need to make a change and explore other opportunities where the existing structure presents you with multiple promotional opportunities and chances for career advancement. However, you must ensure that you do this at the right time and change jobs only after you have fully exhausted all options with your current employer. Serial job hopping often has its own drawbacks. Most employers consider it to be a negative trait and may see you as unstable and unreliable. Employers are even less forgiving if you are a mid-or senior level professional.

5. **Shiny Object Syndrome:**
From time to time, some new schemes or ideas will pop up around you, and everyone around you will tell you that you can easily make money and retire rich if you pursue those routes. These ideas are usually very attractive and there is a high likelihood for you to fall prey to only to realize later on that it was all a scam. Pyramid schemes and many of the 'work-at-home' ads which fill up your inbox fall in the category of scams that you must be wary of. Some ideas will be presented as money doubling initiatives while others may pitch themselves to their victims as the fastest way there is to make money. You need to watch out so that you don't get caught off guard and lose your money to fraudsters. The modus operandi for most of these scams is to present an air of immediacy whereas you must make investment decisions at once or face losing the opportunity, which will only come once in a lifetime. Many of these fraudsters may also contact you via phone calls. If you take the bait and let them prey on your enthusiasm to make money, you will end up losing your hard-earned money and may even face financial ruin.

You should study and verify all investment opportunities that look too good to be true, because they almost always are. Take your time to search on Google, read reviews, or discuss the opportunities with a more knowledgeable person. The best way to invest is to study the track records of the investment vehicle before you invest your money. As I am writing this e-book, cryptocurrencies appear to be the Shiny Object in vogue, and many people are buying into the cryptocurrency frenzy because they the prices of their investments jumped by over 80% within a month without any fundamentals. They have heard stories about the few millionaires who made their money from cryptocurrencies, and due to the fear of missing out (FOMO), they are quick to buy into it even though they do not really understand how it works.

The truth is, by the time these Shiny Object ideas begin to proliferate the media, it is already too late to invest in them. By that time, the early movers, are on their way out, and are selling at astronomical profits. The whole concept of cryptocurrency is not a bad one. But before you put your hard-earned money into it, or into any other wildly attractive investment, you must study and understand what the investment is about, and be clear about how you will make money from it.

CHAPTER FOUR

4.0   More Money... More...

In his 1997 album "Life After Death", the "Notorious B.I.G" sang: *"the more money we come across, the more problems we see."* Although I do not agree that more money will necessarily bring more problems for everyone, I understand the rhetoric and believe that it the statement holds true for many people. Often enough, I have heard of instances where some people got into trouble after they came into some unexpected wealth. Most of these people are quickly drawn into the seedy underworld and get involved in many dangerous and self-destructive habits including gambling, reckless spending, drinking uncontrollably, sexual immorality, keeping late nights, and so on. As soon as there was a change in their financial status, the fact that they could afford to spend money on anything that they wanted makes them also become toxic.

Money is a neutral tool, which reveals its best attributes in the hand of the judicious user who spends and uses it for the greater good. On the other hand, money in the hand of a poor steward, will only bring increased pain and sorrow which is why it is all too common to hear of lottery winners who go broke a few years after receiving their windfall. Those who use money wisely have perfected the subtle art of allocating their income in such a way that their money will always serve them for good.

I recently conducted an interesting survey where I asked people why they want more money. The responses from the survey proved what I had always known: most people work today to earn income, pay bills, and take care of their personal needs, without having any tangible financial goals.

I want you to pause for about ten minutes here.

Answer this question:

"Why do you want more money?"

Close the book, and take your time to think about it. If you can, find a pen and a paper and write your reasons down as clearly as possible.

What answers did you give to the question? Are they superficial and lacking tangible objectives? You do not have a good financial goal if your major reason for wanting more money is to impress others or to ensure that you are better off than your peers. You need to determine the deeper motives behind your quest for more money, because this reason will guide your actions, consciously or subconsciously. You should not work hard and earn money just because the people around you are doing that. Having clear intentionality behind your desire for more money will sharpen your focus and develop the right motivation and drive to achieve your financial goals. Your motivation should be much more than putting food on the table, buying clothes, or being able to afford your rent. There is nothing wrong with having personal goals like paying off debts, saving towards a down payment for your dream home, or contributing towards retirement so that you can retire early. Even though you have these personal financial goals, you should endeavor to have a goal beyond you, one which will impart the lives of other people in a positive manner and benefit people that you may never even meet directly.

This is what people like Bill Gates, Warren Buffett, Bill Ackman, and many other philanthropists who are similarly dedicated to *"the Giving Pledge"* do, whereby they commit to giving the majority of their wealth to charitable causes during their lifetimes or after they are dead, through donations in their Wills. This is a selfless act, and it's a great way of giving back to bless others. Most of these philanthropists have families, and they could have made a choice to pass their wealth down to their children, but they choose to make a difference by giving their money away to people and causes that need them more. The 'Giving Pledge' was started with 40 pledges in the United States in 2010, and by April 2020, there were over 200 pledges from 23 countries around the world. To these philanthropists, more money means more opportunities to be of use in a more tangible way – by being a blessing to others.

I was especially thrilled to learn that Benjamin Franklin is still touching lives 200 years after his death! In his final Will, Franklin left the city of Philadelphia and Boston a gift of 1,000 pound sterlings each, with an instruction that the bulk of the money could not be drawn until after 100 years, and the rest could not be distributed for another 100 years. The money was then to be used to give loans to young entrepreneurs seeking to start a business. At the end of the 200-year period, what was left of Franklin's bequest was close to $7 million!

Ultimately, it is your responsibility as an individual to define what more money means to you. It is up to you to determine whether you want more money to open yourself up to new experiences, travel the world, or make your life a little easier. You may choose to pass your wealth down to future generations or use it to bless others. You could decide to be generous and impart other people around you with the money in your bank account. This is how Bill Gates, one of the world's richest men, chooses to spend his money. Through The Bill and Melinda Gates Foundation, he consistently makes large donations to charitable causes which fight hunger and diseases, and makes life a little more meaningful to others who are less privileged, particularly those in third world countries.

No matter what your situation may be today, whether are still struggling to make ends meet, or you have just started making progress by creating money goals, you have to clearly define what and how you want to spend your hard-earned income, so that as you continue to earn money, you will have full control of where your money goes, and you will be better positioned to achieve and even surpass your overall financial goals.

"Whoever loves money never has enough; whoever loves wealth is never satisfied with their income"
– Ecclesiastes 5:10

4.1   How about a billion dollar in your account?

What is more money to you? To answer this question, let us take a trip to the dream-land for a minute. Let's say $1,000,000,000 was deposited in your account today. Do you know what you will do with all that money? Now imagine that you will have another $1,000,000,000 deposited in your account tomorrow. Will that be enough to take care of all your needs? While you are still in our fantasy-land, now take your mind to the things that give you fulfillment and satisfaction. What are those things?

From my experiences with money over the years, I have come to the conviction that chasing more money will not bring satisfaction to anyone. Rather, contentment and fulfillment come from being satisfied and staying true to those things that are truly important to you. And more than that, you will find out that your greatest joy comes from giving your money out as a blessing to others.

In my book *"The Winners' Ways"*, I defined success as fulfilling your life's purpose and doing what you are meant to do here on earth. If success is what you truly desire, money may be a component of it, but your perception of success in life should not be entirely tied to how much you have in your bank account. When money is at the core of whether or not you feel safe, secure and successful, you have misplaced your priorities. Money may aid, but it does not guarantee happiness. This is why, despite their enormous wealth, people like Adolf Merckle, Christopher Foster, Anthony Bourdain, Kate Spade, to name a few, suffer from chronic depression and commit suicide. The comedian actor, Jim Carrey, famously said: *"I think everybody should get rich and famous and do everything they ever dreamed of so they can see that it's not the answer."* Your Power to Earn is about knowing what is enough for you to take care of your wants and needs, and to also be in a position to help those who need help, without chasing money at all costs or by any means.

Now you know, money is important, but it should never make up the core of your being. Your sense of self-worth must not be based on how much money you have. You need to establish why you want more money and how much is enough for you, so that you can use the excess to bless others. The following are some points you need to keep in mind as you seek out to craft your lifestyle design and determine what you want more money to bring to you.

1. **You already have what it takes:**
I've heard so many people say, *"I will do so, so and so when certain conditions are in place".* For example, *"I will donate to charity, or give money to others when I start making a certain amount of money monthly".* This shouldn't be so. You shouldn't have to wait till you reach specific money milestones before you start blessing others. You can start from where you are today and give what you can afford. Remember that wealth does not change who you are, it will only magnify what you already were. If billionaires are comfortable giving out millions, and millionaires are comfortable giving out thousands, you should start from where you are, and give what you can spare. If giving has not been a part of your normal practice, you can start training yourself by giving out a dollar on a monthly basis to start with, then setting a goal to increase what you give out as you get more comfortable with the act of giving. Giving does not have to be about money alone, you can give your time, share your skills, talents, and experience to the benefits of others. You should gladly do anything you can to make sure that you are also blessing others as a result. John W. Jordan said it best when he stated, *"My philanthropic DNA was inherited from my mother who dedicated her life to the service of others. While she did not have a lot of treasure, she contributed her time and worked tirelessly serving those in need. She also told me that, in her view, the true measure of financial philanthropy is not how much one gives but how much one has left after one gives."* You also have important talents that the world is waiting to for, so go ahead and start giving today.

2. **Think beyond you:**
When all is said and done, life is not going to be measured by the material things you've accumulated, the number of houses you own, the amount of money in your bank account(s) or the number of cars parked in your driveway, but by the number of lives you were able to impart. Thinking beyond 'you' will help you understand that giving is part of the money equation, and that there are millions of people out there in a precarious condition who need your help in order to hang on to hope, and even to life. Bill Ackman once said *"My earliest memories include my father's exhortations about how*

important it is to give back. These early teachings were ingrained in me, and a portion of the first dollars I earned, I gave away. Over the years, the emotional and psychological returns I have earned from charitable giving have been enormous. The more I do for others, the happier I am." Sometimes, you need to put your personal cares and concerns aside and consider what you can do for others to make their lives better. You will realize that helping others, solving their problems, and bringing happiness to them can help make you more fulfilled.

3. **Nothing is permanent:**
   If you don't have what you consider enough today, this does not mean that your situation will be the same in the future. Your story can, and will, change. Experiences of life have shown us that the man who is poor today can become rich tomorrow, and today's tycoon could become broke tomorrow. The tides of life ebb and flow unceasingly. Don't let your current circumstances prevent you from aspiring towards a better future. If you think about it, something that you consider "not enough" actually constitutes a life of luxury to someone else in another part of the world. Some people in other parts of the world who will consider your apartment a palace and your 20-year-old jalopy car, a Ferrari. The excess food that you throw in the thrash may be enough to keep a family somewhere alive for another three days. No condition is permanent. If you give out today, you may be on the receiving end tomorrow. If you don't have today, your story can change, and you may be in a better position to give even more in the future. Life is full of seasons, and the seasons of life change from time to time. When you are in the season of plenty, don't forget to give and bless those who are not as fortunate as you are, because, in your season of lack, you may be the one who is in a position to receive from those who are better off. I will leave you with a quote by Wilson Mizner which says *"Be nice to people on your way up, because you'll meet them on your way down."* What goes around comes around, and more often than you'd expect it to.

4. **Money is a tool:**
   Before you wish for more money, it is always a good idea to think deeply about how you will use the money. Money is an amazing tool, but the effects that more money will generate depend entirely on the owner of the money. You could say that money is a neutral power

which can be used for good or for evil. As a force used for good, money can be an investment that transforms lives. You can deploy your money to go to places that you may not be physically able to go. Your money can travel on your behalf to show people you'll never have the opportunity to meet how much you care about their well-being. You can use your money to build hospitals which will provide access to healthcare for millions of sick people every year. Your money can be used to build schools to educate students, pay off student loans or provide scholarships to struggling students, ensuring that they will graduate without debt. Your money could be the seed capital an up-and-coming entrepreneur needs to create a groundbreaking innovation which will alter our perception of the world and move the world, as we know it, up another couple of steps in its evolution. Laura and John Arnold said *"We view our wealth in this light - not as an end in itself, but as an instrument to effect positive and transformative change."*

How do you view the wealth you want to accumulate? Is your paramount desire to gloat over the vast amounts you have accumulated in your portfolio and revel in the fact that you have more than you need for retirement? I'm challenging you to change your thinking today. Remember that money is a force that wants to be put to work and transmuted. No one profits by storing energy in a box, but, when you find a channel for it to be used, you can make magic! Don't just hoard, or continue to accumulate money. Rather, let it be used as a tool for positive transformation. Your money will thank you, and its rewards will be reciprocally felt in the abundance that will surround you.

5. **More money is not equal to more happiness:**
   What is the essence of having more money? Certainly, more money could mean more choices and opportunities, and a life that's a little more comfortable. With more money, you can buy a better house or car, gain access to better healthcare, and afford healthier food choices. More money may also mean that your children can attend the best schools around and you can take your family on vacations to expensive locations around the world. These material comforts are good on their own, but the truth is that they will not necessarily bring more happiness to you. The mainstream media is replete with stories of multi-millionaires and billionaires who commit suicide

because of the emptiness they feel in life. Richard Branson said: *"Stuff really is not what brings happiness. Family, friends, good health and the satisfaction that comes from making a positive difference are what really matters."* And he should know, considering he's a multibillionaire with massive investments in aviation, real estate, food and beverage, transportation and lots more! He owns properties around the world, yachts, private jets and even a private island! What he wants you to take away from this statement is that accumulating more and more wealth will not necessarily enhance your happiness, but your efforts in spending quality time with the people who love you and making a positive difference in the lives of others is the key to fulfillment and satisfaction, which will boost your inner happiness and bring you serenity and peace.

4.2   Your Salary Is Not Equal To Wealth

Here is a mantra that I'm sure we are all accustomed to: Go to school, graduate from college, find a high-paying job, and save money for your retirement. All our lives, we have been programmed to believe that this sequence forms the path to a successful life. These are good things to strive for, I'll admit, but, by now, you certainly know that they are not all-encompassing. Neither are they guaranteed, for that matter. Life has its quirks, and we often find ourselves in situations that steer us away from this regimen. Layoffs, relocation, government policies, pandemics, and many other unforeseen circumstances often make it challenging, if not downright impossible, to stick to this plan. What that means is that each individual retains a personal responsibility to find his own way in order to build and grow wealth. Over many years of interactions with different people, I have come to realize that although it is great to earn a high income, a salary is not the same thing as wealth. It is not your salary that makes you wealthy. It is what you do with your salary, which, working in tandem with some other crucial factors, will determine whether or not you will be able to accumulate and sustain wealth.

Here is a hypothetical question for you.

Would you rather earn an income of $250,000 per year without any assets or an income of $75,000 per year with zero debt, and an investment portfolio worth over $2 million?

A novice in personal finance may be tempted to pick the higher salary, thinking that high income means more wealth. I will help you figure out the best option by illustrating the situation with a case study of two individuals: Kenny and Kerry

Kenny works as a science teacher in a high school. He is 48 years old, and he started working at the age of 23, after graduating from college with his bachelor's degree. Kenny went to an in-state school, and he was able to complete his college education without debt. He got married and lives with his wife and two kids in the suburbs. Kenny's starting salary as a teacher was $45,000. Through hard work and dedication, he has continuously made progress in his career, and he now earns $75,000 per year. Kenny and his family live a very simple life. They go on a vacation once in two years, they buy used cars, and they paid off the mortgage on their home a few years ago. Kenny's wife, Kara, is a stay-at-home wife who sometimes teaches English online to international students, and makes an average of $15,000 yearly from this venture. This family started investing as soon as they began their careers, putting 10% of their income into their investment account. After paying off their mortgage, they are now in a position to invest as much as 35% of their income. Kenny and Kara are both below 50 years old, but with their modest living on an annual budget of less than $30,000, they can afford to retire and live off their investment portfolio for more than 25 years. They are wealthy.

Kerry is a high-income earner, but he is also a prolific spender. He works as an investment analyst in one of the largest banks in the country. He is 52 years old, and because he took his time to go for an MBA program in an Ivy League college, he did not start his career until he was 30 years old. Kerry owes about $180,000 in college loans. He has had two divorces and is currently on his third marriage. He also has four kids, two from each marriage.

Kerry enjoys living large. He takes vacations twice a year, drives the latest luxury cars, and uses his cars only for two years before buying a new one. He recently bought a new home that cost $1.2 million in an exclusive gated community within the city. Kerry likes designer labels, and he buys expensive clothes, shoes, jewelry, and wristwatches for himself and his wife. All his kids attend private schools, and he makes sure that they have access to anything that they want. He does not budget his money but spends as he earns. His monthly expenses are usually close to 95% of his income, and sometimes he spends more than his income. Kerry and his family live paycheck to paycheck with no financial discipline. If anything should happen to Kerry's job, he will become broke immediately; he cannot survive a month without earning a salary. Kerry is not wealthy.

It is obvious that Kenny is a better manager of money than Kerry. Please note that I have nothing against earning a high salary. It is good to earn as much as you possibly can, but this must not blind you to the other important things in your life or rob you of foresight. Now, put Kenny in Kerry's shoes and imagine how much he could achieve if he applied the same financial discipline to a higher income. He would already be a multimillionaire! Ultimately, how you utilize your high salary will determine whether or not you are able to build wealth. From this scenario, it is obvious that wealth building is independent of your salary. It takes discipline, planning, focus, commitment, and time to build real and long-lasting wealth.

Income and wealth are often confused in our society today. It is possible to meet a flamboyant high-income earner like Kerry and assume that he is wealthy. It is also likely that you will take it for granted that someone who earns an average income like Kenny is not wealthy. These assumptions are based on fallacies and a lack of knowledge about the true meaning of income and of wealth. Your income is the amount of money you receive on a regular basis. This could come from your active work as an employee or employer, the earnings from your investments, or the payments you receive for services you've rendered. Your income is an important tool that can be used to build and grow your wealth, which can be achieved by carefully planning, managing, and deploying your income to wealth-producing investments. On the other hand, your wealth is money you can generate through your investments. Your wealth is measured based on the length of time in which you can maintain your current lifestyle without receiving any compensation from an external source.

The simple message for you here is to ensure that you manage your income properly and use it judiciously to help you build sufficient wealth to take care of your personal needs, and give back to humanity. If you are a high-income earner, ensure that you plan and manage your money wisely. If you are earning less than you deserve, do all you can to change the situation. To carry out an accurate and detailed profile of wealth, you must be able to look beyond outward appearances or the income that a person earns. You need more information than that. What is their debt profile? Can they really afford the lifestyle they are living? Do they have any assets? These are the questions you should be asking. In summary, the Wealth Assessment Quotient is measured based on how frequently and how much an asset can generate sustainable income for the owner, minus any outstanding liability.

4.3   Learning by Example:

Alex owns 10 rental properties which generate $14,500 monthly income. His monthly expenses, which including homeowners association fees, taxes, insurance, and maintenance on the properties, are $4,750. Alex still has some mortgage on the properties, and his total monthly mortgage is $8,525. What is Alex's Wealth Assessment Quotient (WAQ)?

Total Income = $14,500
Total Expenses = ($4,750 + $8,525) = $13,275

Total Net Monthly Income = $14,500 - $13,275 = $1,225

Therefore, Alex's WAQ = **$1,225 or 12.25%**

Note: The higher the WAQ, the wealthier a person is.

CHAPTER 5

5.0   What If Money Didn't Matter?

One of the most effective ways to put things in perspective and understand what your life is really about, is to consider what you'll do if money were not an objective. I've asked many of my acquaintances this question before, and I usually get varied responses, from traveling the world, to starting a charity organization, becoming a scuba diver, motivational speaker, a soccer coach, or going into full-time ministry.

I want you to give the question a shot:

"What would you do if you have all the money you will ever need for the rest of your life?"

Take a minute or two to think about it…

What was your response?

If you have never given this question a thought before, it may seem a little tricky, and you may be unsure of what you will do in this situation. After all, you can't simply resign from your job, go back home, and decide that sleeping, eating, and binge-watching TV shows are how you would like to spend the rest of your life. That will not be productive at all, and you will most likely get tired of living such a life within a few days or weeks.

The purpose of this question is to help you put things in perspective and really understand why you work, why you do what you do, and why you are in your chosen career field. This question will help you connect with your passion, and determine what you are happy and willing to do, even if you will not get paid for it. Most people in your office are simply there to pick up the money the employer promised to pay them at the end of each month. Certainly, many of these people work hard, contribute their best, and sometimes even work outside their regular work hours, but ultimately, their major motivating factor is getting paid. If you don't pay them, they will stop working.

"If money were no longer a factor, what would you do?" is not a question designed to steer you away from work. Rather, it can help you find the exact career choice that is right and most suitable for you. For example, I work as an engineer, and that is where I get the bulk of my income. I also enjoy writing self-help books and speaking to people to bring out the very best in them. If I am offered a lower-paying job which gives me the opportunity to do those things that I am most passionate about, I will definitely consider it. This is because my passion and love will stimulate interest and creativity in what I do, which will naturally boost my levels of productivity. On the other hand, if I were to be paid double of my current earnings to work as a medical doctor, I will vehemently turn down the offer. If I take on a role in the hospital, I will most likely be unable to perform at my best.

Ruminating on this question will also help you consider some other things you can do in your personal life. Let's think about it for a minute. Are we created and born into this world, to grow to adulthood, start working and earn money, only so we can take care of our needs and those of our children? Is that what life is all about? The answer is NO. There is much more to life than to work, pay bills, and retire someday in order to actually commence the fine art of living. During your active work life, you must be able to figure out the other things you can do personally and that you enjoy. With a good dose of planning and determination, you may be able to turn your passions into a thriving business.

I challenge you to ponder a little more on this question:

If money does not matter, would you rather be a:

Sport coach?
Then don't wait, start your sport's academy with your own children.

Blogger?
You should write today, post it online and repeat the same next week.

Teacher?

Start from your home, volunteer your time to teach, and remember that there are many potential students looking for great, passionate tutors.

Pastor?
Create your message, become a Bible study or Sunday school teacher or post motivational videos on YouTube.

Musician?
Write your song, sing it, post it on YouTube, TikTok or other trending platforms.

Author?
What is stopping you? Go ahead, find your topic, and start writing. Create a blog, post your works.

Motivational Speaker?
Create your speech, give the speech to your spouse. Are they motivated?

Politician?
Establish the problem you want to solve, Find a solution, then throw your hat in the ring.

Chef?
Cook at home, cook for friends, participate in cookouts, create your recipes.

Business Consultant?
Find a struggling business that you can help. Give them free advice, and build up from there.

Business Owner?
Test your idea with those around you, do your feasibility study, start small, and keep growing.

You don't have to be perfect to start, you just have to have the interest and the passion to work on it. In the Universe, every life form starts from seed, and your own undertaking is no different. All you need is to take baby steps each day. You can make a start by putting in an hour every day to work to your personal abilities. You have worked eight to ten hours each day for your employer, so putting in one or two hours to build your own life should not be too much to commit to. The reason why I emphasize and want you to work on your passion is to avoid future regrets, where you look back during retirement and say *"I wish I had... I should have... I could have..."* To avoid the shoulda-woulda-coulda's in life, you must work on your passion now when you have the strength, mental acuity and enthusiasm to forge powerfully ahead in order to reach your full potential. Interestingly, the most painful regrets that people have are those of inaction (I should have done certain things), and not those of action. We live in a world of endless possibilities, where the very next minute could hold the answer to every dream you've ever nurtured, so there is really no excuse to not give fulfilling your passion a fighting chance. I know you need to work in order to earn income. But after work, why not spend some time to nurture yourself by working on those things you are passionate about? Believe me; you will be happier for it!

5.1   Passion & Profits

When you come to that crossroad where you need to decide on the career or business to start, you must be able to balance your desire to earn, as much as possible, with doing what you enjoy. You must give both factors your equal attention if you are to achieve the lasting success and fulfillment you desire. If your sole focus is on your potential earnings, while you ignore your happiness or passion for the job, at some point down the line, the job will begin to feel like a chore and you will suffer from burnouts or face dead ends. When you do something for the money alone, you are no different from the mercenaries who fight for causes they don't believe in in order to get paid. Naturally, it becomes sheer drudgery, and you begin to get tired of doing it because money alone is not a strong long-term motivator for humans. On the other hand, if you too much on your passion alone without figuring out a way to turn your what you love into a profitable venture, you will go easily broke and become disillusioned.

I've met and interacted with many business-owners whose businesses were borne out of passion. Usually, they ventured into these businesses to solve a particular problem that's prevalent in society, to provide services that fill a perceived gap or to create products that fulfill some needs. It is good to have passion for whatever you do, but passion alone is not sufficient to build a successful business. The magic alchemy for success is to combine equal parts of your love for the business with the ability to make money from it, and stir the two together with a good dose of patience and determination. The same formula is applicable to your career as an employee. When choosing a career, you need to ensure that you choose what you will enjoy, and at the same time, make sure that you can earn enough money from the career to take care of your personal and family needs. What use will it be to start a business which has no potential to attract customers, create a product that no one needs, or go into a career with no future growth opportunities? There is a very thin line between passion and profit, and just as it is when you are walking a tightrope, you must be able to find the perfect balance to get to the other side. In this instance, the other side is the outcome that is best suited to your personality, skill set, and career objectives.

Balancing passion with profits requires you to gain some important skills and master the ability to use available information to study trends and anticipate the market needs. Jeff Bezos did this successfully when he created an e-commerce giant that made it easy for customers to buy virtually anything they wanted online, from their phones or computers. At a time when people had to go into bookstores to buy books, he started selling books online. Gradually, he added other items, and in the process, he got people addicted to the comfort and luxury of shopping on Amazon.

Mark Zuckerberg recognized the need to stay in touch with friends and families in diverse locations around the world. He solved this problem by creating Facebook, which connected people and made it easy for them to stay in touch with the people they cared about. Before Facebook, you could only communicate with your friends through phone calls, emails or by sending handwritten letters by post. But Facebook revolutionized communication, and now, you can literally send an instant message to anyone, anywhere in the world. Jeff and Mark built their businesses by anticipating what people will need in the future, even when those people were completely unaware that they would have those needs.

Don't bother thinking that you can simply re-invent the wheel by creating another social media website like Facebook, or an e-commerce website that's just like Amazon. These companies have dominated the space, making it extremely difficult for new competitors to come in and take a good bite of the market share. If you are starting out to build a new business, you need to think creatively and build a company that is capable of creating a future that people will be happy to buy into. When you combine future potential with your passion, you will have a successful business. In the same way, if you start out life as an employee, you must study the current trends and ensure that the career you choose is future-proved. For example, choosing a career in an endangered industry will not be a good idea. Before choosing a career in a print newspaper company, you should know that ease of access to online media will make it difficult for the company to survive. If you plan to work as a language translator, you should know that there are apps available now that make it easier and faster to learn and translate languages. Going for a career in the coal industry at this age is a huge risk, because renewable energy sources are getting cheaper, and more people are learning about the harmful effects of coal in the environment. Before you choose your career field, you must be strategic. You must consider all your options critically in the light of current disruptive trends and future potentialities while balancing your passion with the inevitable need to make money.

If you find yourself in a dead-end career, or in an endangered industry, it is not the end of the world. You can turn your situation around for good by reinventing yourself. The following guidelines will help you reinvent yourself and future-proof your earning potential:

1. **Take Initiative:**
   As we noted earlier, the greatest regret for most people is that of inaction. When you find yourself in an undesirable situation, doing nothing is never a good option. In order to get out, you've got to make a move and do something about it. What you choose to do in

such a situation will determine the outcome that you get. Are you the type of person who accepts everything that comes their way as fate or destiny that cannot be changed? Or do you take action and say, *"I am going to change this condition!"* Times and fortune have always favored the brave, and the future belongs to the people who are proactive, who take initiatives, and who will not let the circumstances around them determine their outcome in life. As an individual, you need to continually find ways to reinvent yourself in order to stay relevant in your career or business. Taking the initiative means that you should develop a healthy appetite for risk taking, not being satisfied with the status quo, and doing novel things that will challenge you intellectually and take you out of your comfort zone.

2. **Be Adaptable to New Ideas:**
   Companies that go bankrupt, people that become outdated, or countries that fail to develop are the ones that refuse to innovate, learn, and adopt new ideas. For an organization to reinvent itself, it must constantly innovate and invest in the right technology and personnel that will consistently expand its customer base and keep it at the forefront of industry trends and developments. For an individual to reinvent himself or herself, he or she must be willing to explore and adapt to new and improved ways of doing things. How has your job or career changed over the years? Are you acquiring the new skills that will help you compete effectively in the current and future market place? Uber is disrupting the transportation companies; Airbnb is a threat to the hotel businesses. No one can effectively fight the impact of technological advancements today; the best strategy is to adapt and get in on the game. The key to staying relevant is to disrupt before you are disrupted.

3. **Think Creatively:**
   The power of thoughts cannot be over-emphasized. What you are and where you are today is always a direct result of the thoughts that you nurture and foster. The motivational and self-help space is filled with books that teach you how important your thoughts are in crafting your reality. You can, and should learn to use your thoughts to create the world that you desire. Many people complain endlessly and enjoy finding and discussing problems, from how bad their

bosses or employers are, how terrible their spouses are, to how corrupt the government is. These people usually spend little or no time on finding practical solutions to those problems. A creative mind is a solution-driven mind; a mind that recognizes and acknowledges problems when they exist, but is also ready to focus on how to resolve the issues rather than talking about them. You can use the Power of Creative Thinking to bring positive change to your life. This Power can be used to provide the necessary drive you need to make progress in any, and all, of your endeavors. The good news here is that you have that power within you. Each person has the power in the same measure, and, in this, no one person has a better hand than another. The distinguishing factor is how you use it. So, get creative by deploying this Power as you start on the path to reinventing yourself. You should ensure that you become a creative thinker and a solution provider who is not just interested in maintaining the status quo, but is also ready and willing to stand in the gap by providing new and better ways of doing things.

4. **Invest in Yourself:**
With the rise of the gig economy and the impact of automation and AI, many people are uncertain right now about how to plan for their career progression and what skills will be in demand, or become irrelevant, in the evolving economy. The impact of the Covid-19 pandemic will also see new business models emerge and give rise to a massive tech overhaul in the gig economy. In order to avoid getting edged out in the post-covid wave, you must take a proactive approach to securing your place in the workforce alongside emerging technology. You must invest in yourself by acquiring skills that will help you future-proof your career and put yourself in a position where potential employers can't afford to not work with you. Your investment may include going back to college for an advanced degree, enrolling in online courses to acquire new in-demand skills or getting professional certifications. These days, you no longer need to go through a traditional school system before you can take courses in programming, artificial intelligence, data analysis, Project Management, and so on. Many platforms, including Coursera, edx, Codeacademy, Udemy and LinkedIn Learning are providing opportunities for people to learn and acquire new knowledge at their own pace. If you are not investing in yourself regularly, you may soon find out that your education has become out

of date.   It is important to remember that future-proofing your career does not necessarily mean getting into a technical career. Not everyone is cut out to pursue a career in a STEM field. The economy has always required a diversity of skill sets, and will continue to do so.

5. **Become an Entrepreneurial Thinker:**
Having an entrepreneurial mindset means you must be able to foresee problems before they arise, and you must also come up with creative solutions to deal with potential problems. The entrepreneurial mindset is a great compass for navigating a changing economy. No matter how vastly future careers differ from today's models, the people who have the best chance of coming out on top are those who have initiative, and stay flexible and informed amidst changing times. An employee with an entrepreneurial mindset will easily come up with strategies and ideas that help the employer cut costs, optimize processes, and save time. The entrepreneurial mindset is not exclusive to business owners only. At your workplace, you must think creatively, think outside the box, challenge the status quo, be open to new challenges, and always be a member of the team that is recognized for going the extra mile to make more money for the company.

5.2   Building Multiple Income Streams

In Chapter One of this book, I introduced the Income Quadrant. In that section, I emphasized that the income you make can come from any of the four quadrants. To recap, the quadrants are:

INCOME QUADRANT	
EMPLOYEE	INVESTOR
SELF-EMPLOYED	BUSINESS OWNER

Each quadrant represents a different way to produce and generate income. Many people earn money in only one quadrant; while others earn money from multiple quadrants. The good news is that you can flexibly navigate the quadrants from one to the other. You may be an employee today, and move on to become an investor in the future.

The left quadrants (Employee and Self-Employed) are where you want to be if you prefer to get things done by yourself. Employees earn their income from a job but lack any sort of control over their income. The self-employed have more control but also retain increased responsibility. In either of these quadrants, you will need to work based on requests or directives from other people. I call these quadrants *"the engaging quadrants"*, because they require you to act and stay engaged in order to receive an income.

The two quadrants on the right side (Business Owner and Investor) are the primary paths to financial freedom. You want to be on this side if you want other people to work on your behalf. Business Owners own a system and lead people while investors own assets that produce income. In these quadrants, you are clear about what you want, and provide information that others can execute to get things done for you. I call the two quadrants on the right *"the delegating quadrants"*, because you can use your money or instructions to deploy resources to make money for you. In these quadrants, your income does not depend on active work.

You are free to choose the quadrant in which you would earn your money, but it is advisable for you to earn money from more than one quadrant. It does not matter which quadrant you earn your money from as long as you can maintain your desired lifestyle and can achieve happiness. In truth, there are millions of happy employees, and there are many sad ones as well. Many self-employed people are at their wits end while others are thriving. The same is true of investors and business owners. The fact that money is important is indisputable, as I have often stated, but there must be a certain clarity of thought and intention which surrounds your desire for more money. I have also clarified that it is not wise to make the pursuit of money the driving force for your whole existence. Ultimately, the most important factor is that you are happy with how you are making your money. It is crucial to remember that you are the captain of your fate and your finances. The income quadrant is only a tool which, when used right, can help you figure out where you want to be and chart an effective path to achieving your goals. When all is said and done, you alone must choose the most comfortable quadrant, where you will thrive and fulfill your mission on earth.

We have already established that you can choose any quadrant to work in, but it is in your best interest to ensure that you can generate income from multiple sources. Having two or three jobs as an employee is not the same as having multiple streams of income, because your financial destiny, security, and freedom is still dependent upon the caprices and success of your employers, and you are expending a high amount of life energy to make money. Having one source of income is dangerous as it gives you no control over your income. It is true that you can make a lot of money as an employee but when you stop working or when the business stops, your income stops too and you will be left out in the blistering cold of unemployment and lack. To illustrate, during the coronavirus pandemic in the year 2020, about twenty-five million people lost their jobs.

It is a known fact that an average millionaire has about seven income sources! The good news is that building more than one source of income is no longer as demanding, time-consuming, and expensive as it used to be in the past. The industrial revolution has changed the way things work, and the internet has made it easier, faster, and more affordable to create multiple income streams from the time, energy and skills you already possess. The new push towards less traditional marketing tactics also opens up a whole new world of opportunities for generating multiple income streams. Below are some ideas on how to build your multiple income streams. To make it easy for you, I have categorized these ideas into five (5) main groups.

1. **Make Money through Physical Products:**
   With this method, you can create your product or sell somebody else's.

   - **Affiliate marketing**: *Affiliate marketing* is a great way to earn an income (usually a commission) for recommending products or services to your friends, clients or readers. Once you find a product you enjoy, you can start by creating a professional website, blog or social network where you promote that product and earn a commission from each sale you make. Your sales will be tracked via affiliate links from one website to another. Amazon Affiliates is one of the most popular affiliates programs that you can join. However, because affiliate marketing is extremely beneficial to both brands and affiliate marketers, there are many affiliate marketing opportunities for you to tap into. According to emarketer, 81% of brands and 84% of publishers in the United States leverage the power of affiliate marketing, a statistic that is expected to increase significantly every year.

- **Sell products on online e-commerce platforms e.g. eBay**: If you know where you can get some products at a cheaper price, you may be able to sell those items back with profit on eBay. All you need to do is buy an in-demand product from one store or website, sell for profits on eBay.

2. **Make Money by Providing Services:** The good thing about this method is that it usually comes easier to you because you will be using the skills and experience you already possess to make money.

- **Freelancing:** Freelancers looking to earn more money now have more options than ever before. Freelancer platforms like Fiverr, Guru, Upwork and Toptal help companies find and hire expert freelancers from around the world. People can hire freelancers on these websites to provide a range of services including programming, web, mobile and software development, writing and translation, graphic and web design, video and animation, digital marketing, social media marketing, sales and marketing, admin support, voice overs, virtual assistants, customer service, and much more.

- **Serve others**: Platforms like TaskRabbit, Handy, DogVacay, Postmates and Instacart make it easy for you to make extra income by providing on-demand services such as moving, cleaning, furniture assembly, mounting a TV, fixing household items, pet sitting, grocery delivery, food delivery, and many more for others.

- **Coaching services**: All of us are experts in something. You can set up and run a coaching service and make money in return. There are many coaching services available such as financial coach, life coach, wellness coach, and so on. You can also coach others on particular skills that you have. Fonzworth Bentley, a former full-time valet and butler of the hip-hop artist and producer, P. Diddy, made a lucrative coaching career by leveraging his high level of style, fashion, and upper tier of sophistication as a platform to teach men to look and act like distinguished gentlemen.

3. **Make money through digital products:**
This is my favorite method of generating money from a side hustle. I call it the evergreen method of making money because once your product has been set up and placed on a platform, you can continue to generate income from that source forever.

- **E-books:** One of the easiest and most adopted means of digital learning in this era are e-books. If you have any knowledge that you want to share, it is much easier these days to publish and sell your eBooks via Amazon KDP. Apart from Amazon, you can also explore other direct to e-book retailers such as iTunes, Nook, or Kobo. Some authors also prefer smaller platforms like Gumroad, Leanpub, Kickstarter, and Unbound which provide more off-beat methods of publishing and selling your e-book.
- **Digital Courses**: Teaching an online course is a great way to leverage your skills and earn a side income at the same time. You can create and market your digital courses on platforms like Udemy, Skillshare, Teachable, Podia, Thinkific and Kajabi.
- **Launch your YouTube Channel:** If you have any skill or knowledge to share. You should create your YouTube channel and share your knowledge with the entire world. The higher the traffic you can drive to your channel, the more money you will earn.

4. **Make Money in the Equity Market:**
This method allows you to invest money in existing, well-established businesses. There are tons of opportunities in the stock market for anyone that care to use that means for earning money. You just need to do your research and study the financials of the business you plan to invest in. The reward that you get from your investment in these

businesses is through dividends which the company pay from their profits, either monthly, quarterly, or on an annual basis.

- **Individual stocks**: This involves buying shares of individual companies in your portfolio. You can buy shares in companies like Walmart, Amazon, Microsoft, Uber, Apple, and so on. If you have chosen strong, well-run companies, the value of your stocks will increase over time. This method comes with a lot of risks, but if you do your research properly, you can make money by investing in the stock market.

- **Mutual Funds:** This type of investment provides the advantage of diversification, because, rather than investing in a single stock, you buy into a collection of stocks, sometimes in as much as five hundred companies. You minimize your risks by investing in mutual funds. If you are desirous of earning a stable income from your Mutual Funds over capital gains, you can earn monthly from a Monthly Income Plan (MIP), which is a category of mutual fund that generates stable income through dividend and interest cash flows by investing in lower-risk securities, including fixed-income instruments, preferred shares, and dividend stocks.

- **ETFs**: Exchange-traded funds (ETFs) are a great option because they allow you to quickly own a diversified set of securities, such as stocks, at a low cost. You can also get specific exposure to areas of the market, including industries, countries and asset classes. Like Mutual Funds, ETFs offer diversification opportunities because it is also an investment in several shares of different companies. However, it is more flexible to invest in ETFs because you can easily set your entry and exit price.

- **Bonds**: In their simplest form, bonds are debt obligations. A government or corporation can issue bonds in order to raise capital for a particular venture. The bonds are an interest-bearing security which obligates the issuer to pay the bond-holder an agreed sum of money, at a specific period, with the goal of repaying the principal amount at maturity. It is similar to loaning money to these organizations. In return, you earn a profit from two sources: interest income and capital gains. Bonds pay interest regularly, so they can help you generate a steady, predictable stream of income from your savings. Next to cash, U.S. Treasuries are widely considered to be the safest, most liquid investments on the planet.

5. **<u>Real Estate Investment:</u>**
Investing in real estate is a superb way to increase your wealth in a relatively short period of time. You can make passive income in real estate by buying properties for investment purposes, renting out properties, adding value to your home or other properties that you own, or investing in REITs (real estate investment trusts).

- **Rental properties:** By investing in rental properties, you can make a steady income on a monthly or yearly basis. Your tenants may be made to sign a long-term lease for a minimum of 1 year, and you can also get a monthly rent in return.
- **Airbnb**: If you have enough time to manage it, you can make money by turning your property into a hotel, sort of, by renting it out on a short-term basis to potential tenants. A solidly-booked Airbnb rental may turn out to be even more profitable for you than traditional renting where you rent the property to a long-term tenant. This is because you are usually able to charge more on a nightly basis. Being an Airbnb host holds its own risks as well, such as serious damage to your property by some guests, so it would be wise to carefully consider your options.
- **REITs:** This is a way of making money by buying shares in real estate investment trusts (REITs), which are well established publicly traded companies that own or finance income-producing real estate across a range of property sectors. REITs may include assets in commercial buildings, apartments, resorts, facilities and even mortgages or loans. When you put your money in REITs, you face the same risks as other types of investments. You must do your due diligence or consult with a financial professional in order to ensure that the company you are investing in has a good track record

and that you will be able to generate good returns on your money. REITs are considered a good investment because they provide greater diversification, potentially higher total returns and lower overall risk for the investor.

Closing Thoughts:

5.3   Empowered to Earn

In this eBook, we established that money is an important tool that we all need. It is hard to survive or thrive in this world without money. In Chapter One, I introduced the concept of Income Quadrant. I emphasized that the income you make can come from any of the four quadrants and that you can attain fulfillment and satisfaction in any of the quadrants.

You learned about the money mistakes you need to avoid, and are now familiar with The Five Commandments you must actively live by in order to maximize your Power to Earn. In this book, we also discussed your 'enough' income and you learned that you must be able to establish what your "enough money" is. This will help you determine the level of income that will make you happy and fulfilled, and give you a long-term goal that can help drive your productivity levels during your active work years.

You learned to identify what more money means to you. In the world today, the desire for wealth of many people is driven by counter-productive desires such as the desire to lord their wealth over others or to be admired by their peers. Usually, the story of those whose ambitions are fueled by unworthy motives like pernicious ambitions and greed resemble the Greek legend of Icarus, an ambitious boy who flew on wings of feathers and wax, went too high, flew too close to the sun and crashed to his death as the wax melted in the heat of the sun. If you have read this book and applied the principles to your life, you have learned to apply the perfect balance that helps you achieve the financial goals you are striving for. You will not fly too high in pursuit of vain ambitions; neither will you fly too low by staying in a situation where you do not earn what you deserve simply because it feels deceptively safe.

You have learned how to channel the Powerful Force of Thoughts to create a reality of abundance for yourself. We asked the question: *"If you can get all the money that you want in the world, what would you do with it"?* This helped you elevate your mind and find a higher purpose for your money, which transcended your own personal cares and satisfaction. You also realized that when you practice generous giving and use your wealth to bless others, the Universal Law of Reciprocity brings an abundance of wealth, serenity, happiness and fulfillment back to you. Money no longer holds you in its grip because you know that it is a tool which you are meant to deploy for your highest good and to the benefit of the world around you. A servant who usurps the king's throne is rarely a great or kind leader; rather he unscrupulously exerts his stolen power in a cruel and arbitrary manner. This is what money becomes when you become its slave rather than learning to control it consciously and with good intent – a destructive force which can wreck your life, destroy your relationships and bring pain to those who surround you.

The Power to Earn is a potent manuscript that will guide and motivate you to maximize your earning potential and also help you to achieve the right balance between the time you commit to working and making more money and the time you commit to doing the most essential things in life, such as spending quality time relaxing and bonding with your family and loved ones and time spent on introspection, meditation and self-care. If your earnings are below what you desire, make sure you don't stay too long on an income that is not sufficient to meet your needs. You have the power to make a change, you just need to back up your desire to make more money with the necessary motivation, drive and strategy to improve your income. Remember that everything starts from seed, and men, animal and trees did not appear on earth fully formed. Take your motivation from this to drive your passion from small beginnings to seeking ways to advance and make progress so that you can earn your dream income and achieve your financial aspirations.

One other point to keep in mind is that you do not have to, and should not restrict yourself to a single income quadrant in order to earn your income. Most people focus on just one of the quadrants as the only way they can earn money. If you are a prospective employee who is just starting out, and have been applying for jobs without getting what you desire, you should change your strategy and look into other quadrants. Is it not worth a try to see if you can start your own business, and become a self-employed person instead? To get where you want in life, you cannot afford to stay still. You must keep moving, exploring, questioning and developing strategies until you get what you want. And that is the most important lesson in life, you may not always get what you desire in life, but if you persevere, life can give you what you ask. However, you must make sure you are asking for what you truly want. If you want to become a high-income earner, ask for it, and develop creative strategies and plans that will put you in a position to earn the high income that you desire.

Watch out for Book Two: Power to Save!

You can get it for free by subscribing to my newsletter through this link:
https://landing.mailerlite.com/webforms/landing/c1o7r8